WOMEN, CHANGE, AND THE CHURCH

Into Our Third Century Series

WOMEN, CHANGE, AND THE CHURCH

NANCY J. VAN SCOYOC

Ezra Earl Jones, Editor

ABINGDON   Nashville

WOMEN, CHANGE, AND THE CHURCH

Library of Congress Cataloging in Publication Data

Van Scoyoc, Nancy J 1933-
  Women, change, and the church.
  (Into our third century)
  1. Women in Christianity. 2. Women—United States.
I. Title. II. Series.
BV639.W7V36   261.8'344   80-15739

ISBN 0-687-45958-3

MANUFACTURED BY THE PARTHENON PRESS AT
NASHVILLE, TENNESSEE, UNITED STATES OF AMERICA

Contents

Foreword

In 1984 United Methodism will observe the 200th anniversary of the Christmas Conference of 1784—the date most often regarded as the beginning of the Methodist movement in the United States. We shall pause to remember how the Wesleyan vision of holy love and active piety spread like an unquenchable flame as the United States expanded from coast to coast; how people of all races, cultures, and classes rallied to a gospel offering salvation and demanding good works as the fruit of Christian faith in God.

But we shall do more. Our bicentennial is also a time to soberly anticipate the future, to take stock of ourselves as we move into our third century. Our inheritance is rich in faith and works. It nourishes us but our tasks are now, and tomorrow. The United Methodist Church is large (9.6 million members in the United States), still highly visible and active, but some indicators of our future prospects are disturbing. We shall reflect on and discuss these concerns as United Methodists until we once again catch a vision of ministry and service that is worthy of our past, builds upon our present, and thrusts us again into the mainstream of human life with the message of God's redeeming love.

You, a United Methodist lay member or pastor, and your congregation have a vital role in both the celebration and the search. We in United Methodism must reestablish our identity and purpose through discussion on who we are as United Methodists, what we wish to accomplish, and how we will pursue our goals in the years ahead.

Into Our Third Century, initiated by the General Council on Ministries with the encouragement of the Council of Bishops, is intended to support your efforts. It is an extensive study of selected issues of fundamental ministry and organizational concern to the denomination and a study of the environment in which United Methodism in the United States serves. Over a four-year period, beginning in 1980, 18 separate volumes are being released for your use.

The present book, *Women, Change, and the Church,* by Nancy J. Van Scoyoc is the fourth volume in the series. Books already available are *The Church in a Changing Society,* by William Ramsden, *Images of the Future,* by Alan Waltz, and *In Praise of Learning,* by Donald Rogers. Subsequent volumes will deal with the present realities, future form, and challenges of outreach ministry (mission, evangelism, and social witness), social movements and issues, church leadership and management, nonparish institutions (for example, colleges, hospitals, homes, community centers), local churches as community institutions, ecumenical relationships, ethnic minority constituencies, understanding faith (the role of theology), professional ministry, general agencies, financial support, and polity (the philosophy and form of church government and the organization).

The General Council on Ministries is pleased to offer you this volume by Nancy J. Van Scoyoc on the changing roles of women in American society and the impact of those changes on the ministry of the church. We believe it will help you to understand better the life situations and aspirations of both women and men in our society. Perhaps it will also stimulate your thinking about how the church can reach out in new and caring ways to people whose patterns of living and relating are distinctive or different. Share your reflections within your own congregation, with other Christians, and with district, conference, and general church leaders. Your response will also be welcomed by the members and staff of the Council. You may write to us at the address below.

Norman E. Dewire
General Secretary

Ezra Earl Jones
Editor

The General Council on Ministries
601 West Riverview Avenue
Dayton, Ohio 45406

September 1980

Introduction

As we look toward the future of the church, the far-reaching changes occurring in women's lives are, and will be, profoundly affecting the structures and life of the church. The purpose of this book is to look at these changes, some of their effects, and the implications for the church's ministry.

Life choices for women have increased dramatically in the last 10 years. The multiplying opportunities—and frequent dilemmas—revolve around employment and careers, life-styles and relationships, marriage and divorce, choice to have or not to have children, and the use of free time for volunteer commitments, self-improvement, recreation, and family.

A convergence of factors has produced this rapidly changing picture of women's lives. Recent statistics show that in this country 57 percent of all women over 18 are employed, compared with 42 percent employed 10 years ago. Add to this the decreasing size of families, the increasing divorce rate, and increased life expectancy of women, and it is clear that previous models, traditional roles, and ways of coping and finding meaning in life no longer fit.

Behind the obvious, measurable changes in women's lives is another story—a story that covers the spectrum of individual response to change—the frustration that it is too slow, the attitude that it is happening to others and does not concern them, and the tendency to try to keep it contained in one small area of life while trying to maintain the status quo in the rest of life. Almost always there is the ambivalence about what it might mean for the future. This ambivalence is inevitably part of a time of transition, when women are not ready to let go of some of the things they have long valued, and yet are lured on by the challenge and promise of new opportunities to join the mainstream of the river that is rushing by them.

The church, as it deals with the issue of women's changing roles and assesses where it is in relation to the stream of change, is faced with questions about its institutional life and about the lives and needs of people. I say "people," because anything that deeply affects one-half or more of any group or population will unavoidably affect the whole population.

As women extend their sphere of activity and expand their self-definition, men are forced to ask, "What does this mean for me? How am I affected in my role?" It is like a delicately balanced equation where the various roles and functions in the family, society, and institutions, such as the church, are distributed in a predictable pattern, largely defined by sex. Now that roles are changing and are less sex-defined, the balance has been upset. There are new stresses as we search for answers to new questions. The security of knowing where one fits in has been shaken, and individuals, as well as institutions, are reassessing, reevaluating, reshaping the form of their lives in the community.

There are widely differing levels of awareness about what actually has changed, and differences in conviction about what should change. There are also varying degrees of willingness to act on knowledge and conviction. Before the church can plan effectively for the reshaping of its ministry, if that is called for, many questions must be explored. These are questions about the internal and external realities of women's lives, their relationship to the church, and the prevailing patterns, norms, and attitudes within the church.

A concern for these issues of change and for the effect they are having on the church led to the development of the Women in Transition (WIT) project, an ecumenically based group involved in action research with church women, congregations, and church-related organizations.

This group developed a plan to identify church women who had recently experienced major change in their lives and to collect information about them through questionnaires, psychological tests, and in-depth interviews. The information obtained in the interviewing focused on:

—the events and changes in each woman's life;
—the way she had coped with events and changes in her life;
—the degree of support received from particular individuals and groups;
—the feelings she experienced through this period of change; and
—the degree of satisfaction in the various aspects of her life now compared with 4 years ago.

The initial test of this interviewing design was conducted with 30 women, 35 to 50 years old, who were members of Episcopal, United Church of Christ, and Presbyterian churches.

A corps of 15 women were trained to conduct these initial interviews. Since then, a dozen more have been involved with the project. These are women who themselves have experienced recent transitions in their lives and are active church women, committed to the goal of developing within the church a more responsive ministry to women.

We in WIT discovered during the first few months of interviewing women early in 1979 that many of them were sharing their stories for the first time. They were describing not only the pattern of external events in their lives, but also their deepest feelings about these events and themselves. They were making connections between events and relationships in a new way and learning how their priorities, values, and goals were changing. This information supported our basic assumption that we need to know more about the realities of women's lives before new resources and strategies can be developed to meet the changing needs of women.

Another assumption is that changes in society relating to male/female roles and women's changing image directly or indirectly affect women of all ages, regardless of their role choice. If this is so, it means that every church and every pastor and every layperson's ministry is ultimately affected by changing needs, changing priorities, and changing consciousness of and about women.

The first 30 interviews convinced us that we were on the right track. Women were surprised and excited to think that the church—someone in the church—was interested in knowing what was happening in their lives, and most of them shared freely and willingly. We learned much that perhaps had not been uncovered before. The issues that emerged related to four areas: (1) changes in relationships and in a woman's feelings about herself that are triggered by external changes; (2) blocks or aids to moving successfully through a time of change; (3) the role of personal faith in dealing with change; and (4) the role of the church in the lives of women.

Building on our initial work in the 11 churches in the Washington/Baltimore area, we moved into a second phase of work, funded by the General Council on Ministries of The United Methodist Church. Between June and November 1979, we interviewed over 90 women in urban, suburban, small town, and rural churches from different areas of the country, including Chicago, Philadelphia, Maryland, and Virginia. We studied women aged 21 and up from a wide range of income levels and ethnic groups, including women from predominantly Black and Asian congregations. The churches varied in size from 65 to over 1,000 members. In addition to interviewing individual women, we also interviewed the pastor, or pastors, of each congregation and a group of lay leaders—both men and women.

The women, the pastors, and the lay leaders responded eagerly and cooperatively to the project. They were curious and asked questions: "Why is the church doing this?" "How was I selected to be included in this study?" "What will happen as a result of this study?"

The women in the 12 participating churches were selected from returned questionnaires on which they indicated that they (a) had made a major change in their lives in the last 4 years, (b) were in the midst of a major change, or (c) had not made a major change in the last 4 years. Major change was defined as changes or transitions that involved some significant alteration in their pattern of living. The areas of change included personal relationships, work or career, use of time, state of health, and internal coping or sense of self. The women interviewed were selected on the basis of their having experienced major change and their willingness and availability to be interviewed. No other criteria were used, except age (21 or over). The age range of participants was almost evenly distributed in the three age groups of 21-35, 36-50, and over 50. The average age was about 45 and the range was from 21 to 76.

In addition to being interviewed, the women were asked to fill out two questionnaires—the Myers-Briggs Typology Inventory (a widely used questionnaire yielding information about basic personality type) and a specially developed questionnaire relating to norms of the congregation, perceptions about the church's task, organizational climate, personal support received from the congregation, and opinions on role-related issues. The latter questionnaire was also given to the leaders in each church who were interviewed.

Thus, in order to assess how women are affected by change, we looked at their total lives. In addition to their family and working roles, we set out to examine the recent important events in their lives and their responses to those events, the resulting changes in their lives, and their feelings about themselves. We wanted to know where they found meaning in their lives, who provided personal support, and what was their hope for the future.

Some of what we have found may sound familiar to the reader; some of it may present a picture that differs from the reader's experience. There will be indicators here and clues to pursue as you look at your own congregation and the experience of the women in it; as you share with your wife, mother, daughter, or friend some of her struggles with change in her life; or as you yourself sort through the new choices that accompany a time of transition and bring challenge and dilemmas, pain, and promise.

If you were asked to describe what the pattern of a typical American woman's life is like today to someone unfamiliar with our country, what would you say? A dozen different images would probably flash through your mind. Even if the woman's age, her marital status, or the city in which she lived were specified, it would be difficult to say, with any assurance, what her life-style would be, how she spent her time, what her values and priorities were, or what kinds of critical events had recently changed her life.

We approached each woman in this study with questions about what her life is like, what have been her most important recent life experiences, and how she has responded to them. The answers that we have recorded, and the images of women contained in these pages are incredibly varied. Beyond the fact that they are adult women who have some connection with the church, there is no one common portrait to show what these women are like.

Some are mothers and wives who are very satisfied with their lives.

Some are mothers and wives who feel overburdened and restricted in their choices.

Some are employed for the first time in years and feel their lives are expanding and being enriched as a result.

Others are employed full time and manage a family and long for more time for themselves and their families.

Some are single, some married, and some separated, divorced, or widowed—some feel good about themselves and their situation and some feel frustrated, unhappy, or even desperate.

Some find the church, its activities and people the main source of their support.

Some feel the church does not speak to their deep personal needs or support them in their crises.

How do we select from these stories what is important to know as we look to the future of the church and its ministry with women? We will try to do this by looking first at the nature of the important events and changes in women's lives. Chapter 2 will deal with the patterns of how women are coping with change—what blocks them and what helps them deal with stressful events and transitions. The effects of change will be discussed in chapter 3. In chapter 4 we will look specifically at the role of the church in their lives. In the fifth chapter we will explore some of the implications of this study, and the sixth chapter will provide a guide for reflection on the issues that surfaced.

Acknowledgments

Three years prior to initiating this study of "women in transition," a plan for such a project had begun to take shape through the efforts of James Anderson of the Episcopal Diocese of Washington, and Dale and Gerry Lake, research psychologists in the area of life transitions. They developed the basic research design upon which this study was built. A pilot study testing this design was financed through a grant from the Executive Council of the Protestant Episcopal Church. A grant for continuing research was also received from the U.S. Catholic Conference.

The project staff, Jim Anderson, Bunty Ketcham, Dale Lake, and Nancy J. Van Scoyoc, have been ably guided in their efforts by a steering committee including representatives from The United Methodist Church, the Protestant Episcopal Church, the U.S. Catholic Conference, the United Church of Christ, the United Presbyterian Church, and the Alban Institute. Members currently serving on this committee, along with the project staff, are Celia Hahn, Irene Hardman, Beth Hopkins, Loren Mead, Howard Miller, and

Neil Parent. Administrative support has been provided by the Episcopal Diocese of Washington and the
Alban Institute.

A very significant contribution has also been made
to this project by the 27 women who served as
interviewers. They have been our ears and our
recorders—and have helped reflect to us the important strains and themes of women's lives. We are very
grateful to them for their part in carrying out this
project.

A special thanks is due to Mary Sharer-Johnson,
Vance Johnson, Carla Gorrell, and Susan Bell who
assisted the project team in interviewing the pastors
and groups of lay leaders in the churches, and also to
Jim Anderson, Susan Bell, and Patricia Drake for their
editing assistance and collaboration in writing the last
two chapters of this report.

Finally, we owe much to the women who have so
willingly cooperated with our study and who have
shared so many important events and reflections with
us. We thank them for their contribution toward
expanding our knowledge about women in the church
and hope they have been affirmed by the opportunity
to share their stories.

CHAPTER 1

Patterns of Change in Women's Lives

With warmth and wit Alice told of her experiences of the last few years—how she was almost overwhelmed with kindness from friends and family during a recent serious illness and hospitalization and how she lives with the knowledge that the disease may recur at any time. She continues many of her former activities, living to get the most from each day. She has been very active in civic organizations and in her church. She says she does a lot because there are fewer younger mothers to help; so many of them have jobs outside the home. She is distressed that the PTA is floundering in spite of her efforts. Her family has been quite close but doesn't get together very often since her mother died. The critical events of the past few years have been deaths in the family and illness. Alice is 48 years old. She has lived in a very stable community for over 20 years and is proud of having been an active member in her church for all that time.

Another woman, whom we will call Helen, lives in a highly transient metropolitan area. She said she felt like a "displaced person" when she and her family moved there 4 years ago. Her husband was busy with his work and unaware of her extreme loneliness. An already shaky marriage began to crumble, and last year she and her husband were divorced. She has had to look for a job after several years away from the job market and is still struggling with her lack of confidence that she can do the job and with feelings of guilt about not giving more time to her two children. She remains a fringe member of the church but has found very little support or help there during the painful transition she is making. She observes that "the teachings of the church could support the rebuilding of a new life." Because of her basic faith in God, she believes that she will "come out on the other side a whole person."

These two women have had very different major changes in their lives. One story focuses on physical conditions—illness and death—and the other on internal struggles and relationships. But for both the pattern of living has changed, and they both have experienced some of the effects of the changes in society.

Nature of Changes

Everywhere we visited—in transient communities, in stable communities, in small and large churches, in cities, and in the country—change is affecting individual women and it is affecting families. Not all change is sudden and traumatic; some is gradual or anticipated as natural life transitions.

Four out of 5 women who returned our initial questionnaire indicated there had been some recent major change in their lives. Each of the women interviewed checked the events that had occurred in her life in the last 4 years on an "event list" divided into these categories: financial, primary relationships, recreation and creative activities, sexuality, work and career, religious life, health, education, and a miscellaneous category. The events that were most significant in contributing to change in her life were then explored in detail in the interview. Events most frequently checked were in the "primary relationships" category; next were those in the area of work and career. Though women responded in nearly equal numbers across age groupings, each age group had its own characteristically common events and kinds of change.

Women 21 to 35

In the 21 to 35 age group women are primarily concerned with transitions related to marriage, motherhood, and career.

Unmarried Women. The few single women interviewed (less than 1 in 6 in this age group) all lived in their parents' homes. Their overriding concern was to establish themselves in a satisfying career that would provide them with financial security; and none of them was interested in marriage or considered it as a possible solution to her financial problems. All except one had lived away from home for at least a year and then returned home; none had any immediate plans to leave.

Consider the situation of Janet. It was difficult for this young, single woman to leave her home for a first teaching job in another city, but she was proud to be on her own, able to budget her money, and become independent. It was a great shock to have her contract terminated after one year and be forced to return home to look for another job. Her best friend had been married, and they are not as close as before. She stated that her parents are understanding, but she seldom talks with anyone about her problems. She does not have a ready support system. Now that she's back home, she has trouble budgeting her money and scheduling her time.

For all of the single women interviewed there was some degree of tension in their living at home with parents—a difficulty in making a transition from their dependent "daughter" role. The fact that all of these young, single women lived with their parents may indicate that those who do live independently are not often active church members.

Married Women. The place of paid work is a central focus in the lives of many younger married women. Many opt to pursue a career and delay starting a family for several years. When they leave jobs to start families, they leave behind whole support systems and the source of many feelings of self-worth that being employed brings. These women also expressed guilt feelings, because they had given all the financial responsibility for the family to their husbands.

Financial security is an important issue and leads many young mothers back to the work force. Yet, whether women seek jobs outside the home by choice or economic necessity, the 56 percent who are employed feel especially he ambivalence of dual roles and work hard to do both justice. They are fortunate if their work is personally satisfying, their families are doing well, and their marriage is healthy and fulfilling. If so, their own needs may be fairly well met. If not, they may be using all their energy to cope with the day-to-day realities, and have little time or energy for seeking help or initiating a real change in their circumstances.

In crisis, such as divorce, they may seek help. The most recently divorced women in our study were in this younger age group. Their areas of change will be considered later in this chapter.

Women 36 to 50

Between 36 and 50 a woman is likely to be caught in the cross currents of demands from family members who are experiencing their own transitions. This is where, as one woman put it, "We feel caught between our kids' problems and our parents' problems and don't have a chance to think about ourselves."

At about the same time a woman is experiencing the stress associated with a teen-ager who is trying new behavior, she is very likely to be experiencing new demands from an aging parent and possibly the stormy times of a husband's mid-life crisis.

Most often mothers and daughters assume primary responsibility for daily problems with children and parents regardless of other time pressures. They perceive this to be their role and simply do not expect fathers and sons to share equally with them in these responsibilities.

All of these transitions around her occur when a woman is also apt to be reexamining meaning in her own life and asking, "What am I going to do with the rest of my life?" This is often a period of reevaluation, and it seems to be truly a "mixed bag."

Employed Women. Though most women seek employment for economic reasons, the other satisfactions that come from developing one's talents through paid work have become very real incentives for some women. Women already working outside the home, we found, tend to continue even after the immediate economic need has passed, i.e., children finishing college.

In the case of Margaret, her work is becoming increasingly important to her, and after 8 years she is being recognized for her personal achievements. The children are nearly grown, and her increased salary is a great help in meeting college expenses. Her husband, however, is beginning to feel that the personal rewards are more important to her than her relationship with him. In the beginning he had "allowed" her to work. As long as she looked at it that way, it was O.K. with him. Now he thinks she must choose between working and being his wife. This conflict in their marriage, precipitated by her role change and satisfactions from developing herself outside the home, have caused them to reevaluate seriously their marriage. For Margaret, it means struggling with these questions, Do I need to make myself such that he won't leave home? How much do I risk? Do I knuckle under to be someone I'm not?

These are the kinds of questions many women ask as they weigh the costs and rewards of taking on new roles.

Unemployed Women. Only 1 out of 4 women interviewed in this age group was *not* gainfully employed. Half of those who weren't employed had had recent serious illnesses or had been nursing a close family member through illness. The rest were either considering paid work (with considerable ambivalence) or had no financial need to work.

When a woman who has never been employed or has been out of the job market for 10 years or more, reaches the age of 35 to 40, she often asks, "Should I look for a job?" "Do I want to get a job?" or "Is there anything I can do for which someone will pay me?" We found the most ambivalence among women in the higher socioeconomic levels. Where economic necessity is not a prime motivating factor, it seems harder to "take the plunge" and radically alter a comfortable life by taking on a paid job—even though a woman may be restless and dissatisfied with her use of increasing free time.

As her family responsibilities diminished, Jane, a woman of about 40, took on a major responsibility for Christian education at her church. She realized with some chagrin that she was doing what churches often pay a professional director of Christian education to do. Jane told the interviewer that she would like to be paid but didn't know whether she really deserved it. When she has thought of looking for a job, with her limited experience in paid work, she says, "Women's jobs seem too boring." Yet, she thinks that if she had a real job, her time would be used better. She cannot decide on goals for herself and is reluctant to risk failure. Though Jane finds her work at the church rewarding, she is well aware of the difference her role as volunteer layperson makes. She says, "It's exciting working with clergy on projects—but they go home to wives who cook dinner. I have to cook dinner myself."

Ambivalence about roles and lack of confidence in their abilities make it difficult for women to alter the direction of their lives at this stage. The relative rewards and demands of volunteer work and paid work are important factors in the decisions women make as they plan their use of time and set goals for the future.

Women 50 and Older

If the transitions of the middle years, 35 to 50, seem to raise the basic question, What am I going to do with the rest of my life? the transitions of the post-50 years are largely concerned with a process of reconciling to the events of life and the patterns and directions established in earlier years.

The dominant changes for this age group were illness and death. Nearly 75 percent of the women over 50 in our study cited illness (their own or that of family members) and death among the most significant events in their lives. The other areas of significant change focused around retirement, their own or their husband's, and various changes in relationships, such as children leaving home, marrying, or divorcing.

Illness, Death, and Shrinking Families. The burden of care for ill family members—husbands, parents, husband's parents, brothers and sisters, children and grandchildren—was great. Their own illnesses and health problems were equally as common. In describing their own illnesses, the women associated many of their ailments with the stress in their lives. These health problems ranged from hypertension to serious skin conditions to heart attacks and followed closely the patterns of change in their lives.

Almost half of the women had recently mourned the death of a loved one. Their families were getting smaller—brothers, sisters, and parents dying and children moving away. When parents died, this often was followed by a decrease in the number of family get-togethers. The women talked about children being divorced as often as they talked about them getting married. One woman, in describing her own sense of loss at her daughter's divorce, said, "It was like burying a son."

Though losses, illness, and trauma predominated as important events during the later years, the "shrinking" of the family also meant, for many women, that finally *their* time for fulfillment had come. After nurturing and caring for others for many years, or juggling both job and family responsibilities, there were often lessened demands from others and more time to pursue interests that had been shelved for many years. Though about half of the women between

50 and 65 were employed, many of those who were retired or had fewer family responsibilities found this to be "the best time of their lives." Many traveled more, pursued hobbies, or just enjoyed "taking it easy."

Retirement and Marital Problems. Common among the married women over 50 were marital problems or difficult adjustments when their husbands retired. The marital problems may have existed earlier but were easier to ignore when a woman was busier with other things or had a more active life with other family members. Of those whose husbands had recently retired, about half viewed it as a positive transition and enjoyed having more time to spend with their husbands. The other half viewed it as a turn for the worse and described their feelings in strong terms— "retirement is horrible" or "sometimes you climb the walls."

Often, women who had been happy with jobs or volunteer activities and felt that they could choose what they wanted to do and liked to do experienced unexpected restrictions and demands when husbands retired. Some said their husbands wanted them around all the time; they had not developed hobbies or interests to fill their time. Also, many had to nurse husbands who were ill.

None of the women over 50 were recently divorced or considering divorce. They were generally not making decisions to change the course of their lives at this point, but were adjusting to difficult circumstances, finding enjoyment and satisfaction where they could, and following, more or less, a course plotted earlier.

One exception to this pattern was Doris, a woman just over 50 who a few years ago began to feel "swallowed up" by family demands. She cared for her husband's parents for two years before they died. An adult son recently moved home to live. There were demands from her own aging mother. She also helped with the family business, which required fairly strenuous physical work. For some time she felt unappreciated but had difficulty expressing her feelings. Several months ago she began seeing a professional counselor and is struggling with making some changes in her life that will help her meet her own needs and use her talents in a new direction. She is in the middle of her struggle to change and knows that the future holds possibilities she never considered a few years ago.

Divorced Women

Of all the critical events in a woman's life, probably none is more traumatic or has more far-reaching effects than marital separation and divorce. They involve changes in financial status, primary relationships, sexuality, work and career, leisure time, religious life, and health.

Our study showed that 1 in 6 women between the ages of 21 and 50 was divorced; there were twice as many in the 21 to 35 age group as in the 35 to 50 age group. All except one of the divorced women were employed, and the majority of them had children.

It would be difficult to say what had changed most in the pattern of their lives. Some said moving back home to live with parents. For others, becoming financially independent and self-sufficient seemed most difficult and most significant. Those who moved into full-time employment usually found it to be a major adjustment.

However, the accompanying changes in relationships and the women's feelings about themselves, though more difficult to assess, were probably the most dramatic. Most of the women told how they had moved through the painful feelings of self-doubt, guilt, and failure to a point of acceptance that they had done what they could to save the marriage and to a sense of confidence that they could make it on their own. For most, the worst internal struggle came before the divorce. (For one woman the process of working through self-doubt, guilt, and failure lasted 17 years before her marriage terminated in divorce.) After exploring the alternatives, clearly these women viewed separation or divorce as the only possible decision they could make. As one woman put it, "I had to do it for my own self-preservation; it was either go down with him or leave."

Relationships within their families changed as a result of divorce—with their children, with their siblings, and with their parents. One woman told how shortly after her own divorce, her parents unexpectedly divorced also. Several older women related that their children's divorces had affected their own lives, and in two cases, the parents experienced serious marital problems after their daughters were divorced.

What all of these facts and observations about the changes in the lives of separated and divorced women who were interviewed cannot tell us is what it has been like for the women who dropped out of the church at this point. We can only imagine that their stories might differ from those of the women who are active in the church.

Even among those interviewed, some who had left the church returned after they had made their transition, feeling that they could come back on their own terms. The data show that a much higher percentage of separated and divorced women indicated a decline in attendance at worship, church activities, and use of pastoral counseling services than was found to be true in the total group. Surprisingly, the smallest increase in all church activities for divorced women was in the use of pastoral counseling services. In fact, there was an overall decrease in use of such services by divorced women.

Where did these women find support? How did they respond to the changes in their lives? What made the difference, as they moved through stressful situations and transition, between barely surviving and emerging with some degree of confidence in themselves and their ability to cope with the change? These questions will be considered next.

In this chapter we have described what we found happening in women's lives and have examined the patterns of critical events and change. Next we will look at their response patterns and ways of coping and explore what tends to help or hinder them as they move through stressful times.

CHAPTER 2

Response to Change

Through all the women's stories—Alice's illness and Helen's divorce, Janet's struggle for independence, Margaret's and Jane's role conflicts, and Doris' struggle with the overload of family demands—and many more outpourings of ordinary and extraordinary troubles and triumphs, certain themes were repeated over and over. The single fact that initially emerges is that these women have survived some very stressful times and done so, for the most part, with a calm acceptance of what life has brought their way. This section looks at how women respond to change —their sense of responsibility, their source of personal support, and the helpfulness of sharing problems.

Patterns of Seeking Help

When asked, "Did you seek help from your pastor?" the reply often came, "No, but I know he's there if I ever need him," or "I didn't go to a counselor because that's something you do as a last resort—and if I can just hang in there, things will probably straighten out in a few months."

Of course, there were exceptions to this pattern, but it was pervasive enough that our first answer to the question, How are women coping? is:

Women are coping quietly with the stress and change in their lives.

Women seem to feel that in many situations they ought to be able to handle their troubles and stressful times without seeking special help. Some women who want to get help for a particular problem look first for "permission" from their husbands. Sometimes the husband says, "No, you don't need outside help, I'm your best counselor." A woman might be aware that she needs help, but asking for it seems difficult. In this sense, women are "coping quietly."

There is evidence that many women make assumptions about the kinds of problems with which pastors will be helpful. For example, some women who are struggling with a marital problem automatically assume the pastor will not be helpful or understanding. On the other hand, women usually assume that pastors will be helpful in times of illness and death.

The obvious external events of illness and death are the ones where help is almost automatically given by pastors, members of congregations, friends, and family. The less obviously stressful situations, such as career change or dissatisfaction, difficulties with relationships, loss of friends or families through moves, and especially internal conflicts and emotional stress associated with role changes, often are treated as private matters. The women did not often look for help from others to cope with these situations.

In our initial questionnaire, women were asked about the use of pastoral counseling services. A large majority (66 percent of women) checked "is not frequent now and never has been." Only 15 percent indicated relatively frequent use of pastoral counseling; 14 percent checked "more frequent than before" and 5 percent checked "now less frequent than before."

Lay professional counseling help was sought less often than help from pastors. This help was usually sought in extreme circumstances and in most cases was judged to be very beneficial.

Assuming Responsibility

Along with a tendency to keep their troubles to themselves women tend to feel a responsibility for taking care of others' needs and to continue taking on other people's problems, while giving their own needs lowest priority. *Responsibility* is the key word here. Women feel responsible for husbands, children, parents, in-laws, friends, whether there are others who can share the responsibility or not. Here are examples of what we heard:

"My brother-in-law died and I took leave from work to take care of my sister-in-law's children." (*I* am responsible for my in-laws.)

"While I was going to school and working part-time, the hardest thing was keeping up with chauffering my kids to ball games and music lessons and the orthodontist." (*I* am responsible for taking care of my children's needs.)

"My mother is getting senile and I'm the only one in the family to care for her—I only have one brother." (*I* am responsible for my parents.)

"My daughter is divorced and has to work, so I have to care for my grandchildren." (*I* am responsible for my grandchildren.)

"My husband retired and needs me at home, so I had to quit my volunteer activities." (*I* am responsible for my husband's happiness.)

"I knew I wanted to stop working when I had a baby, but now I feel I've given up so much. My husband had to take a second job and hardly ever sees the baby." (*I* am responsible for parenting our baby.)

There is, perhaps, no surprise here. Whenever there is a need in the immediate family or extended family, the mother, wife, daughter, or female relative has nearly always been the one to jump into the breach, because the male breadwinner has usually been occupied with earning a living. The interesting thing to note is that now over half of these women are employed outside the home, as compared with women 50 years ago, or even 15 years ago.

Yes, many of these women have new roles *and they have kept the old roles as well.* Rather than changing roles, they are assuming more roles and responsibilities. They are homemakers, wives, mothers, volunteers, *and* breadwinners. They do not want to let anybody down. If they drop some of their church activities, ask a neighbor to take over the car pool, or ask their husbands to make the next trip to the orthodontist, they feel guilty. They feel that they should do it all. And so when the stress begins to build up, they just try harder, do not complain, and cling to some satisfaction in being needed everywhere—at home, church, and work.

Maybe they didn't intend it to be this way. We heard such comments as: "I was only going to work long enough to pay for the children's college, but you get used to the money, you know, and I like my job. . . ."

Or, "My husband was very supportive when I started working and had agreed to share the housework, but he's so busy and tired when he comes home I hate to ask him!"

Or, "I thought I would quit my volunteer work at church because I'm so tired when I get home at night, but the church is important to me and I just can't let them down."

Along with having high expectations of themselves in meeting others' needs and demands, women generally have low expectations of others in terms of being helpful. This is especially true concerning male family members—husbands, sons, and brothers. They do not expect husbands to share equally in visiting the sick, in listening to children's problems, or in offering support to a divorced family member. Often in describing support people who helped through a difficult time, women automatically discounted the possibility of a male family member helping "because he's a man."

Sources of Support

Our assumption was that receiving support from others—individuals and groups—was an important positive factor in helping a woman cope. For each of the major events discussed, each woman interviewed rated various individuals, groups, or organizations associated with it as to helpfulness, 1 being very unhelpful and 7 very helpful.

The generally "helpful" ratings given in all the categories confirms the fact that clergy, professional counselors, family friends, and groups provided important support to women in transitions or stressful times. A closer look at these ratings, however, will bring to light some differences between categories of helpers and between categories of women (see Figure 1 on pages 40 and 41).

Highest Ratings. Among the different categories of individuals and groups, the one receiving highest ratings was "friends." This is not surprising, since the title "friend" itself implies a positive relationship. Even so, over 7 percent of friends received "unhelpful" ratings from employed women.

Lowest Ratings. Family members generally received lower ratings than any other category. This included husbands, children, parents, siblings, and in-laws. They were mentioned far more often than other support people. Since family members are present to some extent during most important events, they are likely to be counted more often as significant persons, whether they are helpful or unhelpful. Homemakers and part-time employed women both rated family lower than other support people. However, full-time employed women rated clergy lower than any other category.

Homemakers and Employed Women. A consistent difference occurs in the ratings made by employed women and those who listed their primary occupation as "homemaker." Homemakers gave higher ratings to clergy, professional counselors, friends, congregations, and other groups than the full-time employed women. The one category where this was not so was in the ratings given to family members. Here it was reversed to a slight degree, with 66.8 percent of homemakers giving positive ratings to family members and 72.5 percent of full-time employed women rating families positively.

In general, employed women gave lower ratings in all categories except family members than did full-time homemakers. It may be that employed women have become more self-reliant and less reliant on getting help from others. Another factor may be their lack of time. With a job and duties at home too, there simply is less time available for maintaining close relationships with others. This may also account for their higher ratings of family members, their most easily accessible support people.

Part-time Employed. The least helpful ratings were given to professional counselors, family members, and clergy by part-time employed women. Families received 35.8 percent "unhelpful" ratings and counselors and clergy about 25 percent "unhelpful" ratings by part-time employed women. This may be accounted for by the fact that part-time employment often occurs for many women during the initial stages of a major transition when the family experiences the most conflict over the changes and adjustments that are required. It also may occur at the same time a woman is reassessing her volunteer role in the church and experiencing the ambivalence this often brings. It raises the question, How are clergy responding to women who curtail church activities when they seek employment outside the home?

WOMEN'S RATINGS OF SUPPORT PEOPLE AND GROUPS

Ratings were made on a scale of 1 to 7; 1—very unhelpful, 7—very helpful, 4—neutral. (Percentages for unhelpful equal the sum of ratings of 1, 2, and 3; percentages for helpful equal the sum of ratings of 5, 6, and 7; percentages for neutral equal the 4 ratings.)

KEY

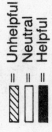

= Unhelpful
= Neutral
= Helpful

Women's Occupation

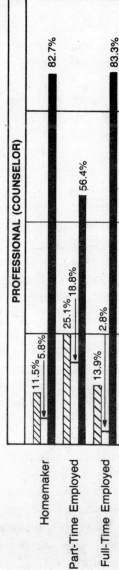

CLERGY

Women's Occupation	Unhelpful	Neutral	Helpful
Homemaker	5.4%	6.9%	87.7%
Part-Time Employed	11.0%	25.0%	64.0%
Full-Time Employed	18.4%	14.3%	67.3%

PROFESSIONAL (COUNSELOR)

Women's Occupation	Unhelpful	Neutral	Helpful
Homemaker	11.5%	5.8%	82.7%
Part-Time Employed	25.1%	18.8%	56.4%
Full-Time Employed	13.9%	2.8%	83.3%

0% 25% 50% 75% 100%

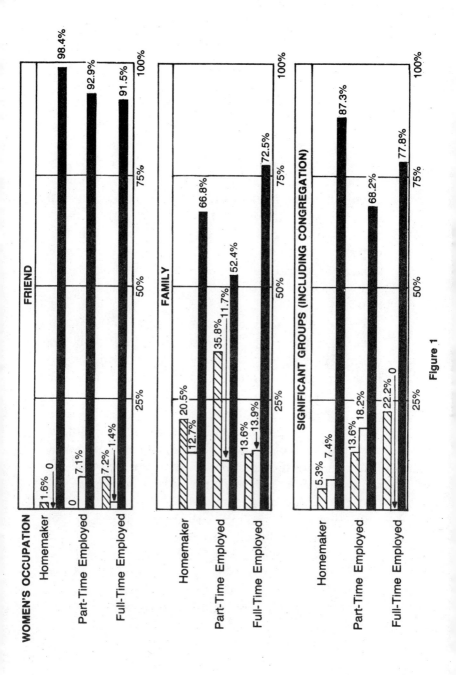

WOMEN'S OCCUPATION

FRIEND

Homemaker — 1.6% — 0

Part-Time Employed — 0 — 7.1% — 92.9%

Full-Time Employed — 7.2% — 1.4% — 91.5%

98.4%

25%   50%   75%   100%

FAMILY

Homemaker — 12.7% — 20.5% — 66.8%

Part-Time Employed — 35.8% — 11.7% — 52.4%

Full-Time Employed — 13.6% — 13.9% — 72.5%

25%   50%   75%   100%

SIGNIFICANT GROUPS (INCLUDING CONGREGATION)

Homemaker — 5.3% — 7.4% — 87.3%

Part-Time Employed — 13.6% — 18.2% — 68.2%

Full-Time Employed — 22.2% — 0 — 77.8%

25%   50%   75%   100%

Figure 1

Defining Support

A further question also remains in terms of defining the word "support." It is apparent that there is more than one level of support—there is verbal support and there is support in the form of action. A friend may say, for instance, "I'm sorry to hear that your mother is ill and had to move in with you—let me know if there's anything I can do." And then there is the friend who says, "It sounds like you need a break from caring for your mother. I'd be glad to come by for the day on Saturday so you can take some time off."

Verbal support may indicate there are people "waiting in the wings," to help out if things really get tough. However, if these potentially helpful persons receive no direct request for help, because a woman finds it difficult to ask, their support will not be felt. Such was the case of the woman whose husband "approved" of her returning to work and said he would help at home; she rated him as very supportive. But when questioned further, she indicated that she didn't ask him to help around the house, so his patterns of helping changed very little. And she continued to cope quietly with the extra stress in her life caused by fulfilling two roles.

How do women cope when they receive no significant support from others? Usually, one of two ways. They may rely on their own internal resources or, not having either internal or external support, may just get by without coping very successfully.

Turning Point for Change

At every stage in life, women tend to accommodate, adjust, and do whatever is necessary to meet the demands put upon them. But sometimes another pattern was heard from women who, for various reasons, had recently begun to focus on their own needs in using time, in finding a direction for their lives, or in dealing with a stressful situation. Sometimes this happened through paid employment, a return to school, or a divorce. Some were free choices from among several viable alternatives. Others were forced choices, such as economic need or loss of husband. Sometimes this shift of focus took the form of a reexamination of the traditional roles of homemaker, wife, mother, and volunteer as ways of expressing one's particular gifts and talents—rather than simply as duty and service to others.

When a significant change in course takes place for a woman, it often involves breaking out of a pattern of rote-role behavior, such as accommodating the demands of others. We found that the rote-role behavior frequently includes a woman's denial of the negative reality of her situation, resulting in increasing symptoms of stress and feelings of helplessness. We looked for incidents or processes by which women were able to break through these blocks effectively.

From both the process of the interview itself, and from the information women shared with us about their experiences during the last few years when they acknowledged stress, we learned:

When a woman recognizes the stress and change in her life and identifies where the pain is—particularly when she shares that with another person—an almost certain release and relief are experienced. This is often the first step toward using resources for helping herself.

The Interview Process. It has already been mentioned how willing, and often eager, women were to tell their stories. One woman said, "I've answered a lot of questionnaires, but this is the first time I've known something to happen as a result." Most women acknowledged that it felt good to know someone was saying, "Your life and your experiences are important, and the church cares about what's happening to you." Knowing this helped establish a climate of trust and openness for the sharing of many private experiences and feelings.

Another important factor was the interviewers' interest and commitment to the goals of the project. Though they were trained with careful guidelines about maintaining neutrality, not inserting their own values, and not trying to give solutions or help, their ability to establish rapport with those being interviewed was a great asset in terms of the depth and quality of the information they were able to obtain.

Many women had evidently come to the interview intending to share in a limited way and surprised themselves by sharing more. The most painful experiences are often the most private ones and, therefore, the most difficult to share. Frequently, an interviewer heard something that had never been told to another person, or that had been carefully hidden and half forgotten. At times, a woman discovered connections or a new understanding about the relationship of events in her life that seemed very helpful. Often at the end of the interview, the participant said something like, "I didn't realize so much had happened to me in the last 4 years!"

Our interviewers observed that the *process* of recounting important and stressful events and times of transition, and then reflecting upon what had blocked or helped in coping as they moved through that period, was generally a powerful experience. Sometimes, saying for the first time, "It's really been hard, and it still hurts," is a recognition point that may be painful but offers a very real release. The impact of the interviews could not be measured, but certainly the women's responses indicated that it had been a significant experience for them.

Acknowledgment of Stress. There were many interesting examples from the stories women told that demonstrated an obvious positive result after acknowledgment of stress. The most dramatic of these related to relief of physical symptoms. Some physical symptoms reported were severe—migraine headaches, severe backache, spastic colitis, unusual skin disease. In all these cases, when the sufferer acknowledged to someone else the load of stress she had been quietly carrying, there was an amazing relief of the physical symptoms she had been experiencing. Even when the stressful situations were unchanged, the release of feelings seemed to increase the ability to cope. In these cases the release and relief of sharing with another person were tangible and unmistakably connected to the recognition and telling.

Another pattern emerged from our data regarding sharing with another person. When a woman is in a "stuck place" or seems to be blocked, cannot resolve her problems, and seems unable to utilize the resources available to help her, she may respond to another person who listens to her and says, in effect, "Yes, it sounds like you need help." The person listening does not try to solve her problems, but she recognizes and acknowledges the problems and affirms that there are resources for finding help.

We found no important differences among the three age groups in the likelihood of their experiencing the value of problem or stress recognition. Some women in the older age group had carried their burdens quietly longer than the younger women. For both there was strong evidence that sharing with an "intermediary," a nonjudgmental support person, could be a key first step in giving up some of their burdens.

Conclusion

Usually by the end of the interview, it was fairly obvious how well a woman was dealing with the events in her life. Often, the sum total of the events recounted presented a picture of a time of testing in the woman's life. The process of recalling the events of the past four years gave a woman an opportunity for reflection and a chance to see how the different pieces fit together, the parts played by different people, and the pattern of her response during a time of transition. This appeared to be a valuable process for many women.

Finally, in answer to the question, What made the difference for you in your ability to cope with the events of the past few years? some women very quickly answered, "My faith in God is what got me through." Others gave the credit to the support of husbands, family, or friends. A number of women took a few minutes to ponder—as if the realization was new, or a startling thought to share—and described something like a turning point when they knew that they could make it because of their own inner strength. They acknowledged some help from others but were not wholly dependent on it.

Other women, like Alice, who accepted her personal illness and held fast to the same values and standards, even though there were indications of the world changing around her, never seemed to question or to ask, "Why is this happening to me?" They seemed to maintain a steady unquestioning style of persevering through change, using the guidelines they always had. These were usually women in stable situations.

Those who gave others the credit seemed to say, "I never would have made it myself; the events were too overwhelming." They presented a modest, self-effacing picture of reliance on others. Interestingly, their stories did not always fully bear this out. The facts sometimes showed that they were quietly making the difficult decisions and meeting crises, while accepting very gratefully the help and support of others as well.

Still other women neither accepted unquestioningly, nor gave all the credit to others for helping them through difficult times. These women shared some of their intense internal struggles and saw no easy answers for the future. Yet they seemed to be less concerned for the outcomes of external events, because of their increased confidence in themselves. Margaret was not sure of the outcome of her marital difficulties during the affirmation of her new career role, nor did Doris dare to predict how she would set a course for herself amid overwhelming family demands—but they were both confident of being on the right track, and they found their personal faith a sustaining force, as well as their newly found self-confidence.

CHAPTER 3

The Impact of Change

In addition to examining the process of change in women's lives, their ways of coping, and their support systems, we were interested in assessing the general impact of change in all the areas of personal concerns. It is our assumption that the events that had, in the words of questionnaire, "significantly altered" her pattern of living, would have an effect on a woman's feelings about herself and her level of satisfaction in different areas. This might be a negative or a positive effect.

Ratings of Satisfaction

At the end of the interview each woman was asked to think about the various aspects of her life—financial, personal relationships, recreation/creative activities, attitudes toward her own sexuality, work/career, personal religious life, educational growth, and health—and rate all of them according to whether they were less satisfying or more satisfying now as compared with four years ago. Generally speaking, women rate most areas of their lives as more satisfying now than before. Yet in most of the ratings there is a great deal of variation among individuals in each area.

SELF-DEVELOPMENT SCALE
RATINGS OF SATISFACTION COMPARED TO 4 YEARS AGO

Ratings were made on a scale of 1 to 7, from least satisfying to most satisfying; 4 is neutral.
(*—lowest rating in each row; **—highest rating in each row)

	Single	Married	Widowed	Divorced	Total Sample
Financial Affairs	4.60	4.83	2.86*	6.33**	4.74
Primary Relationships	5.67	5.31	5.00*	6.00**	5.38
Recreation/Creative Activities	4.78	5.21	4.14*	5.83**	5.06
Attitudes Toward Own Sexuality	5.13	5.07	5.00*	5.67**	5.10
Work/Career Life	5.10*	5.33	5.17	5.67**	5.32
Personal Religious Life	5.90	5.98	6.29**	5.83*	5.93
Educational Growth	6.00**	5.19	5.00*	5.50	5.30
Health	5.30	4.89	4.29*	6.33**	5.01

Figure 2

High and Low Ratings. Perhaps of most interest are the differences among the different marital status categories. Figure 2 gives the average for each marital status category in each of the eight areas. The widest variation between groups is in the area of financial affairs, which divorced women find to be much more satisfactory than before, and widows find to be least satisfactory of all. Divorced women in general have the highest ratings of satisfaction in all the categories except personal religious life and education. Widows, on the other hand, score lowest in satisfaction in all areas *except* religious life, where they score higher than married, single, or divorced women.

This consistent pattern of response is worth noting, because it is a good indicator of how women feel about the *direction* their lives are taking. It indicates that for divorced women life seems better after working through the difficult times in their marriages, but there remain unmet needs and unresolved questions in their personal religious lives. From their individual responses, we can identify that some of this conflict comes from violating the perceived norms and teachings of the church and being unable to find ways in the church to deal with these feelings.

The widows are an older group, all over 50, and perhaps feel, to a greater degree than others, that they are the victims of circumstances and less able to change the course of their lives at this point. The greater satisfaction in personal religious life is more typical of the older age group regardless of their marital status.

Single women show less satisfaction in the area of work/career than any other marital status group and greater satisfaction than any other group in terms of educational growth. This measure of satisfaction echoes what they relate about their lives, their concern and struggle for financial independence, and their focus on education as a means of career development.

Specific Areas of Change

To fill in the picture of how we found women responding to change, we will look briefly at each of the areas of events and add some notes about particular situations.

Finances. Changes in financial status were both positive and negative. In some churches where the income level was relatively high it was mentioned infrequently. In lower income groups where it was a more important factor, there was a higher percentage of employed women.

A primary financial concern for many in the under 35 age group was buying a home. Increased financial need often means that these women assisted, sometimes reluctantly, by working. These were most often women with young children. In the middle group from 35 to 50, expenses of raising a family were paramount.

If finances were adequate, older women seemed to enjoy using their money for travel more than ever before. There were almost always changes in the financial situation accompanying retirement. Either a woman's retirement or that of her husband usually meant a reduction in income. However, little dissatisfaction was expressed about the effects of reduced income. It was expected and planned for, and often the needs for spending were reduced at the same time.

As mentioned earlier, one exception to the older women's general satisfaction about income level was the situation of widows. One widow stated, "Our retirement income was adequate until my husband died, and then the company annuity stopped. During all those years of his working for that company, I never knew this might happen." This reduced income often meant that a widow had little choice but to live with one of her children.

With younger married women, as well as with single and divorced women, there was a desire to have some degree of financial independence. This was often translated into more than just seeking employment; it meant aiming for rewarding, well-paying work—what could be termed "career orientation."

Personal Relationships. Changes in this area had less to do with significant changes in the physical situation than they did with changes in feelings and emotions. Loss of relationship, whether by death, a move, or divorce, was probably the most traumatic of all events. A number of women admitted that they had not dealt adequately with some losses, because they had not allowed themselves to grieve, either because they were too busy with other demands or because they felt they had to "be strong" for the other people who were depending on them. For instance, in two very tragic instances of loss of a child, it was the mother of the child who said she could not afford to break down, because other family members were breaking down and needed her to be strong.

Children leaving home, getting married, and getting divorced were all situations that required dealing with a sense of loss. There was a mixture of pride and sorrow as women told of children marrying and moving far away and starting their own lives. They accepted this as a normal and desirable occurrence. If the children or grandchildren had serious problems, however, the mothers again tended to become involved.

Changes in relationship with spouse were mentioned frequently as important events. Very often these were related to external events, such as death or serious illness in the family. There was no one predominant kind of response pattern from women, either to positive changes or to negative changes. Positive changes often meant that a couple grew closer because of some kind of external stress. Sometimes it happened as a result of a woman's changing and deciding to share more openly her feelings with her husband. Whatever the source of the desirable change, as one might expect, it greatly enhanced a woman's feelings of well-being, confidence, and ability to cope.

For many women, not only were family relationships important, but also significant were changes in relationships with friends or the loss of friends. When long-time friends terminated or tapered off a relationship unexpectedly and without explanation, losses were felt deeply.

Recreation and Creative Activities. Children leaving home and retirement were the principal changes that increased the amount of leisure time a woman had. Little mention was made of recreation and leisure activities before the retirement years. At that point, women talked about more time for vacation and travel, as well as the pursuit of hobbies and handicrafts.

Very often improvement in the relationship with a spouse resulted in the couple spending more time together sharing interests or taking a special vacation together. Relief of stress in general seemed to free a woman for more recreation and leisure time.

When a few women talked about pursuing "creative" activities, they did it usually in the course of a job. One woman turned her creativity at cake decorating into a lucrative business. Another woman over 50 had been a "closet painter" for years, and finally at the urging of her daughter began showing her paintings. Her work has received good critical reviews, and she is now selling her work.

Volunteer activities and creative activities underwent the same fluctuations, corresponding to the amount of free time a woman had.

Work and Career. Some aspects of employment have been dealt with in other sections. Whether or not a woman holds a paying job influences almost every other aspect of her life—her ability to maintain some degree of financial independence; her role as a friend, a wife, a mother, or a daughter; her time for hobbies or social activities; the extent of her volunteer commitments and participation in church activities; and her own feelings of self-esteem and confidence.

Some women worked at paid jobs who wished they did not have to. Other women worked at unfulfilling jobs and wanted something better. Many women who stayed home wanted to find rewarding jobs outside the home.

Whatever their work situation, if they were married, family relationships and events were usually considered at least of equal importance as job-related concerns. It was much more likely, however, that an employed married woman would give family concerns priority over job concerns.

Sexuality. Items on our event sheet under sexuality included changes in a woman's own sexual behavior and her spouse's as well as change in feelings about herself as a sexual being. In addition to divorce, separation, and marital problems as major causes of changes, those most frequently discussed were decline of sexual activity attributed to spouse's lack of interest or impotence.

A majority of both married and divorced women indicated having better feelings about their sexuality than they did 4 years ago. This often came as the result of working through problems in relationships. Sometimes it seemed to be part of the more general increase in feelings of well-being, self-acceptance, and self-worth.

The greatest indication of negative change came from women over 50 and was related to decline in sexual activity. These were not problems they shared easily, and the need for counseling help in some cases was very obvious. But with sexual problems more than any other, the unspoken rule was to cope quietly.

Health. There were far fewer improvements in health than there were negative health changes. The connections we found between health problems and stress have already been mentioned. Illnesses of family members were mentioned considerably more often than the women's own illnesses. Women tended to treat their own illnesses lightly, except in cases where they had been disabled for a long period of time, or were very seriously ill. Not infrequently a woman's health problems coincided with other family problems and took second place in the attention they received.

A health-related problem—overweight—was discussed frequently. With most women it was seen to be connected with their emotional state. Some admitted overeating out of frustration or even "to get back at" a family member. One source of help found to overcome the problem was groups such as Overeaters Anonymous. An attractive young woman who credited her success in losing weight to Overeaters Anonymous described it as a significant support group, because it helped her feel better about herself.

Education. About 5 percent of the women interviewed listed themselves as students. They were engaged in college work after being away from it for a number of years. All except one were employed as well. Others were currently taking courses but did not list themselves as students. More than half of the students were married women. One woman had returned to school but lacked tangible support from the family and quit. Others had recently completed work for a degree.

A prime motivation for going back to school was advancement in jobs already held. All found it difficult, but they also found rewards in a greater awareness of all kinds of issues as well as in their own personal growth.

The last area, that of religious life, will be dealt with in detail in the next chapter.

CHAPTER 4

Relationship with the Church

In looking at the role of the church in women's lives, an important distinction needs to be made between a woman's involvement in congregational life, the particular role of the pastor in her experience of the church, and her personal faith and belief in God. Since our criteria for selecting participants in this study required that they claim membership in a congregation, this is the prevailing common denominator and the one we will consider first.

Women's Involvement in Congregational Life

Even though the extent of women's participation in church activities varies considerably, our assumption is that these are women who find church membership of some value in their lives. The majority of women are fairly active in church activities. Those few who appear to be "fringe" members still value some aspect of church membership. Their belonging to the church seems to involve an affirmation of "religious values" and family tradition, but with no high investment in participating in a particular church's activities.

Levels of Participation. We attempted to assess levels of participation in various aspects of congregational life, as well as changes in that participation over the previous four-year period. The initial questionnaire through which the women were selected for the study included 4 questions about their church activities: (1) attendance at worship services, (2) adult education programs, (3) fellowship activities, and (4) use of pastoral counseling services. They were asked to indicate whether their participation was frequent or infrequent or whether it had increased or decreased in the past 4 years during their period of change. (Figure 3 shows responses.)

1. *Attendance at worship services.* This is the area of highest participation. Most attend frequently; 23 percent had increased attendance and only 9 percent show a decrease.
2. *Adult education programs.* Participation is lower here than in fellowship activities or attendance at worship. About 25 percent show an increase over the last 4 years, while nearly 40 percent show a decrease or infrequent participation in activities.
3. *Fellowship activities.* This area shows the highest percentage of increase—35 percent. A near majority, 44 percent, show frequent attendance, and the rest divide between infrequent and decreased attendance.
4. *Use of pastoral counseling services.* This is considerably lower than any other category. Sixty-six percent indicate infrequent use and only 15 percent seek pastoral counseling frequently. There is an increase over the past 4 years of 14 percent, and 5 percent decrease.

Responses to Initial Identifier Questionnaire

Following is the section from the initial questionnaire dealing with the level of participation in church activities and increase or decrease in those activities. The percentages answering in each category are listed at the left.

1. My attendance at Sunday worship services
    9% is now less frequent than before
    3% is not frequent now and never has been
    65% continues to be frequent, or almost every Sunday
    15% has become more frequent
    8% is far more frequent than ever before

2. My participation in adult education programs at my church
    9.5% is now less active than before
    29% is not active now and never has been active
    37% continues to be fairly active
    15% has become more active
    9.5% is far more active now than ever before

3. My attendance in the various fellowship activities of my church
    10.5% is now less frequent than before
    10.5% is not frequent now and never has been frequent
    44% continues to be fairly frequent
    23.5% has become more frequent
    11.5% is far more frequent than ever before

4. My use of pastoral counseling services
    5% is now less frequent than before
    66% is not frequent now and never has been frequent
    15% continues to be relatively frequent
    11% has become more frequent
    3% is far more frequent than ever before

Figure 3

This initial picture from the questionnaire is borne out by the interview data. The women we talked to tend to be very active rather than "fringe" church members. The small groups they belong to in the church seem particularly important to them, as does the warm and friendly climate of the congregation. It seems to be an important center for social activities, especially for older women. Bible groups, prayer groups, and small study groups provide the most important opportunity for a sharing of personal concerns; these are usually family concerns (problems with children, illness, death, and so forth), rather than concerns about jobs, marital relationships, or personal role conflicts.

Leadership Roles. Women have definitely assumed a larger share of leadership roles in the church in recent years. In every church we visited, women share nearly equally in chairing various administrative committees and groups and most have at least one woman who serves as a lay worship leader. In some churches more women hold leadership positions than men. In fact, more than once we heard the comment, "Women run this church." There still are some lay roles that remain the province of men, such as membership on finance committees or superintendent of the Sunday school. This varies from church to church. In our interviews with men and women lay leaders in the churches, there was consistent verbal support given to equal inclusion of women in leadership roles. Where sex-role divisions remain, as chairpersons of key committees, women lay worship leaders, or equal representation of men as Sunday school teachers, few opinions were offered to explain why certain old sex-role patterns continue. Aside from designated leadership positions, women almost always are more active than men in performing the great variety of volunteer tasks, including teaching Sunday school classes and serving on many committees.

Of the 12 United Methodist churches in the study (3 of which were in the same rural circuit), 2 churches—1 urban and 1 suburban—have women pastors; a third has a woman assistant pastor. The proportion of active women compared to men is even greater in these churches.

Response to Life-Style Changes. Negative response to congregational involvement centers around the real or imagined nonacceptance of changed life-styles (*i.e.,* divorce) by the congregation and unrealistic expectations regarding volunteer contributions. When a woman's situation changes, such as having children or working outside the home, the expectation of the congregation regarding her contribution of volunteer time does not always change.

Women feel considerable conflict and guilt over turning down requests for help with church programs when family or work demands interfere. One woman said, "I don't think the church understands the realities of life for working women; there just isn't time or energy to do everything!" Some acknowledged having to overcome guilt feelings during their early experiences with the church, and were only recently beginning to feel more comfortable as church members. These early experiences produced fear of "hellfire and damnation" and feelings of unworthiness or of never being good enough.

Intersection of Church and Personal Concerns

Although belonging to church remains an important part of their lives, many have a feeling of vulnerability in sharing too much of themselves with the church. It appears that the church represents a haven in a confusing and troubled world, a needed voice of authority and supporter of cherished values, while, at the same time, for some it represents unreachable standards and reminders of individual imperfections and fallibility. Thus, while drawn to it as a refuge and a symbol of safety, women are careful to protect themselves from possible rejection and uncomfortable guilt feelings by sharing only the most acceptable parts of themselves.

This, then, is an important learning from our interviews with church women:

> There are some particular concerns that are felt to be appropriate or safe to share with members of the congregation and other areas that are taboo or not "important" enough to bring into the sphere of the church. Unwritten norms seem to dictate what parts of a woman's life intersect with the church.

This area of intersection between the church and the whole of a woman's life and personal concerns will usually include some, but not all, of the areas of significant concerns. Figure 4 portrays this intersection of the 2 spheres. Illness and death are the 2 areas most commonly shared in the church.

The following comments from women indicate that though some feel the church is too far removed from everyday concerns, they desire to understand better how the message of the gospel can be translated to speak to these concerns:

A young career woman: "Most of my life is spent in the secular world, and my concerns there seem to be unrelated to my faith."

A recently divorced woman who cannot find a support group in the church: "The church is backward and unhelpful in helping single adults deal with issues relating to sexuality."

A widow: "The pastor uses too many 'family' examples in sermons—single parents should have their situation treated as a way of life rather than a disaster. Pastor and people need to be at the same point."

A formerly active church volunteer: "After 15 years I felt a personal need to do something that was valued with a paycheck. After starting work, I began to feel distanced from people in church when I was no longer available for every job that needed doing. The church seemed really indifferent to my lack of participation, in failing to recognize my situation had changed."

A recovering alcoholic: "AA became a substitute for church. I needed a spiritual frame of reference and the church was interested in social issues, not personal issues."

These comments are from women who have strongly felt needs in areas that have not been recog-

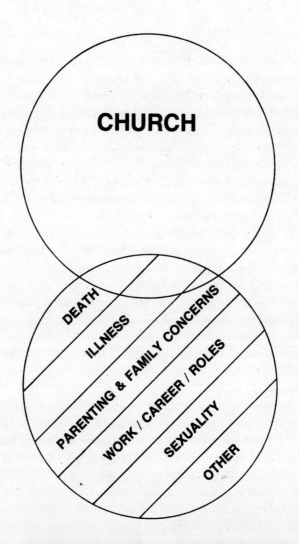

CHURCH

DEATH

ILLNESS

PARENTING & FAMILY CONCERNS

WORK / CAREER / ROLES

SEXUALITY

OTHER

PERSONAL CONCERNS

Figure 4

nized and responded to in their experience of the church. Certainly, the general climate about each of these issues varies from church to church. In a few congregations there is open discussion of issues such as abortion and divorce. However, the prevailing norms and attitudes of people in a congregation are communicated in diverse ways and very often the message is that issues of sexuality, marital stress due to role changes, career concerns, and so forth, do not belong in the sphere of the church.

Churches Respond to Issues

We were interested in finding out the views and attitudes of women and the church leaders in the areas of the church's task, the organizational climate, personal support received in the church, and feminist or role-related issues. All the lay leaders and the women in the United Methodist churches answered questions in all these areas.

The feminist and role-related questions pertained to abortion, two-career marriages, use of feminist language, acceptance of a woman pastor, mothers of young children working outside the home, and the responsibility of mothers for nursery and Sunday school.

Generally there was agreement between women and leaders in each church. On a few questions, however, disagreement was noted. Congregations differ greatly on the issue of abortion. In about half, the leaders' views differ from the women's. Some women favor elective abortion for married women while the leaders in their church are against it, and in other churches the leaders support elective abortion, while the majority of women are against it.

On all the feminist area questions there was at least one church where the women disagreed with the leaders. However, there was no clear pattern of either the women or the leaders being more liberal.

A look at the averages of all those who responded (see Figure 5) shows no strong general agreement or disagreement with the issues. On most of the questions respondents are quite divided—many strongly for or against and fewer uncertain. So the averages that cluster around "uncertain" often include widely varying individual opinions.

The responses in the 3 churches where there are women ministers are very highly accepting of women ministers. Excluding these 3 churches, the average of the responses is much closer to undecided on the issue of acceptance of a woman as a pastor.

The pattern of responses in the other 3 areas of the questionnaire showed: (1) ratings of congregations in terms of personal support is generally high; (2) in the area of the church's task, there was ambivalence in response to questions of affirming spiritual affairs over physical or worldly affairs in human life; and (3) the climate of the churches was felt to be friendly, open, and encouraging of involvement, with the pastor and congregational leaders open and receptive to comment and criticism.

In general, then, the picture this gives us of the 12 congregations is that they are fulfilling well the role of providing a friendly, "supportive" Christian commu-

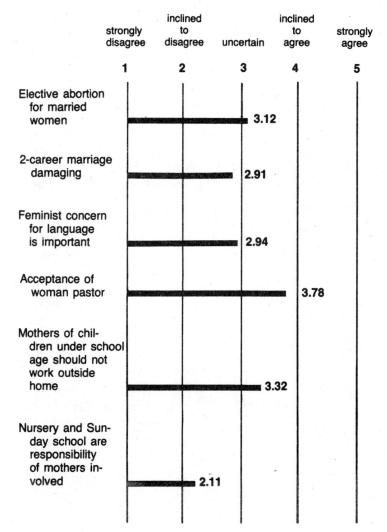

Survey Questionnaire

(Responses on role-related and feminist issue questions)

	strongly disagree	inclined to disagree	uncertain	inclined to agree	strongly agree
	1	2	3	4	5

Elective abortion for married women — 3.12

2-career marriage damaging — 2.91

Feminist concern for language is important — 2.94

Acceptance of woman pastor — 3.78

Mothers of children under school age should not work outside home — 3.32

Nursery and Sunday school are responsibility of mothers involved — 2.11

Average of Total Responses from Women Individually Interviewed and Lay Leaders

Figure 5

nity. In terms of issues reflecting and dealing with the role changes in society and in perceptions of the church's task, considerable uncertainty and widely differing views were discovered.

Role of the Pastor

If we look again at the diagram of the intersection of a woman's personal concerns and the church, the particular role of the pastor(s) of a congregation needs to be added to the picture. In Figure 6 we represent the pastor's role as a smaller circle intersecting some additional personal concerns. It might intersect fewer concerns. It would also vary in size for different individuals and in different congregations. In some cases it might be larger than the church. There is an almost endless variety of ways this might be depicted in such a diagram.

Many factors affect the role of the pastor and his/her relationship with individuals in any congregation. Some of these have to do with the particular talents and gifts he/she brings to the role and others relate to the perceptions and expectations of the parishioners. Of course, there are additional factors too, including the "givens" in any church situation.

First, almost without exception the women had a high degree of respect for their pastors. Few negative opinions were expressed. Previous ministers may have been criticized, but the present ones were regarded as competent, conscientious in fulfilling their duties, and generally liked and admired. Some were enthusiastically praised.

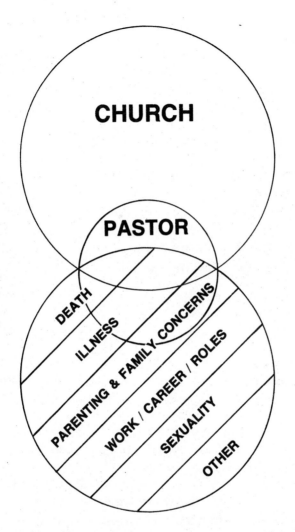

CHURCH

PASTOR

DEATH

ILLNESS

PARENTING & FAMILY CONCERNS

WORK / CAREER / ROLES

SEXUALITY

OTHER

PERSONAL CONCERNS

Figure 6

Several factors seemed to be particularly important in shaping the pastor's role and present ministry in the congregation and with individuals: (1) length of pastorate, (2) approachability and availability, (3) perceptions or assumptions about pastor's skill and what the role includes, and (4) initial experiences with pastor and observations of his/her ministry.

Length of Pastorate. Three of the pastors in our study had just moved to their churches within the last 2 months. Two others had been in their congregations for 1 year. This meant that generally the women in those congregations did not know them well or were reserving comment until there had been more opportunity for interaction. Their expectations seemed to be cautious, and they were willing to "wait and see." In churches where pastors had been serving longer than a year, the women obviously felt they knew the pastor better and the way she/he functioned in her/his ministry. This did not necessarily mean, however, that a woman felt more open to share her personal concerns with a pastor she knew better. It did mean that the pastor's style and particular gifts for ministry were better known.

Generally, women are most comfortable seeking help from a pastor they have known for longer than a year. One woman who had been struggling for several years with a gradual transition from full-time home-maker to "employed homemaker" to "career woman," thought about taking her problems to her pastor for several years before she finally did. It took her that long to believe and to trust that he would listen to her concerns with an open mind.

Approachability and Availability. Some pastors simply were "easier to talk to" than others, or were approachable at one level but not at another. As one woman said, she enjoyed discussing theological issues with her pastor but would not take her personal problems to him. Availability of time was another factor. If a pastor was, *or seemed to be,* very busy with administrative matters, a woman might be reluctant to "bother" him with her particular concerns. Approachability would have something to do with length of pastorate, but probably related more to personality and the image projected. The women pastors in our study were viewed by most of the women interviewed as being very approachable. About one in particular we heard comments like, "I feel I can go to her any time of day or night." Personal warmth, understanding, and spiritual insight invited sharing a wide range of concerns.

Perceptions and Assumptions About Pastor's Skill and Role. Some pastors are viewed primarily as administrators or preachers—the leader of the congregation—and most are highly regarded in this area. Looking at the total sample, there does not seem to be as much confidence in their skills as counselors. Some women say, "If I need real counseling help, I will go to a professional counselor outside the church!" This may be because they feel the pastor lacks the training or time to do intensive counseling. Another possibility is that some women simply prefer to take personal problems to someone outside the church, for reasons of anonymity if nothing else. Some pastors are perceived as being very skilled as counselors, and this often (though not always) has to do with their ability to relate the principles of faith to the women's problems.

Initial Experience with Pastor and Observation of His/Her Ministry. One comment we frequently heard from women was, "Though I've never gone to him for help, I'd certainly feel free to go to him if I ever needed to." (Male pronouns are used here, because this comment was heard in relation to male pastors.) This seems to indicate a confidence in the pastor as a counselor, coming from other positive experiences of him in his role, from personal observations, or from the role image he has in the congregation.

This kind of comment, however, raised other questions. What kind of need would prompt the woman to seek his help? Or what could pastors do that would encourage women to go to them for help? There were women who said they would go to the pastor if they needed him, who had already described a series of stressful events and difficult situations that would have sent someone else knocking on his door long before. The difference in whether or not the pastor's help is sought must have to do with factors inherent in a woman's personality as well as in her perceptions about the role of the pastor and of the church. In any case, the role of the pastor is a crucial one during times of change and provides a promising area for further exploration.

Personal Faith

The role of the pastor and congregation in a person's life are related to the basic undergirding of one's own personal faith, which we found for many women to be the chief element in their ability to deal with all that life brings. This backbone of their strength to cope is formed and nourished from many sources—from their own roots and family influences, from their everyday experiences and relationships, and from their reflection, meditation, Bible study, and prayer. This is represented in Figure 7 by lines coming from different directions outside themselves and feeding into the center of their being. There may be other sources as well. These lines that support and shape their lives intersect through all the layers of their daily concerns.

The extent to which the church and the pastor are the sources of this strength varies. At times they seem to be quite distinct and separate from a woman's reliance on her personal faith. Belonging to a visible Christian community seems to be important, regardless of the degree of direct support felt in terms of personal concerns. For some this direct support came from the church. For others, the deepest concerns were private and only shared with God in prayer. It is as if membership in the church makes a statement to others that "I am a Christian; I believe in God," and yet for many their faith and their spiritual journeys are internal, personal parts of their being that are not actually a part of their experience in a congregation, but a separate, corollary part of their lives.

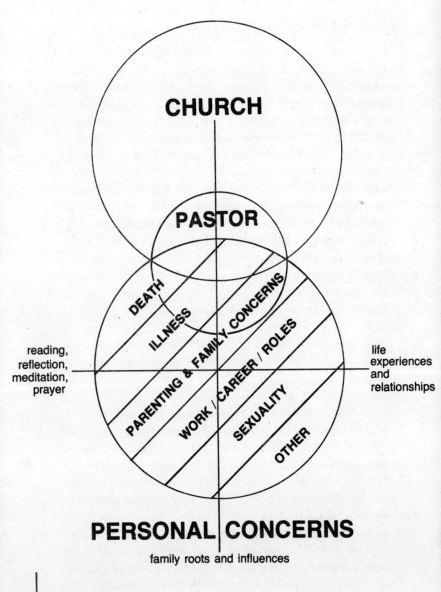

CHURCH

PASTOR

DEATH

ILLNESS

PARENTING & FAMILY CONCERNS

WORK / CAREER / ROLES

SEXUALITY

OTHER

reading, reflection, meditation, prayer

life experiences and relationships

PERSONAL CONCERNS

family roots and influences

＋ = PERSONAL FAITH

Figure 7

Some testimony to this comes from women who have had a profound "religious experience." One such woman told how her life has been affected since such an experience. She now relies totally on the Lord, and it is this faith that supports her through everything. She was never an "every-Sunday" worshiper and at the time of the interview had not been to church for 4 months. She likes the pastor and the services, though she doesn't like the teacher of her class. Church just does not seem important to her, though her faith is.

Another woman's marriage was on the verge of breaking up when she and her husband attended a conference with a charismatic Christian group. They became "born again" Christians, and their lives have been transformed. They still attend their former church but do not share their experience with members of their congregation.

One of the most moving stories shared with us was that of a woman who had been quite ill with a rare disease. She was being treated at a research center, and the doctors could not determine a program of medication that would promote healing and relieve her pain. After much suffering, she experienced an unaccountable, sudden, and nearly complete remission of symptoms. It changed her life dramatically and became for her a time of profound spiritual renewal. The quality of this was so intensely personal that she found it difficult to share. She tried to tell her minister but could not share the whole story. Her family knew some of what she was feeling and were affected by it, but mostly she kept it to herself as something very rare and precious and carefully guarded—perhaps for fear

of not being understood by others. It was as if she were
waiting for the opportunity and the right context to
put all the pieces of her story together, and the
interview helped her do that. She wanted to do it in her
church community but somehow did not feel free
enough to do so.

Not many people have such a dramatic experience.
Yet, we heard over and over the accounts of how
personal faith and prayer were greatly relied on for
support. The interactions with members of the
congregation and the pastor were often somewhat
removed from matters that concerned a woman most
deeply. One woman put it this bluntly, "God comes
first; not the church." The spiritual life, the inner
journey of faith, is simply another dimension of
existence that for some (maybe most) takes place at
another level and that paradoxically does not connect
directly with church activities or the kinds of things
women talk about with their pastors.

Church's Response to Various Events

What events, then, *are* in that area of intersection
between women's lives and the church and pastor? As
we examined the different categories of events and the
support people most often associated with these
events, we found that pastors and congregations are
most involved and helpful in situations of death and
illness. These are what might be termed "public
events," and most of the participants automatically
turn to the pastor and congregation for support. This
support is felt in terms of practical help, as well as

support through prayers, visits, and telephone calls.

Women told how church members not only visited and cared for them when they were ill but also insisted on bringing food daily and caring for the family. Having this kind of care lavished on them was usually a new experience, and some felt overwhelmed by the kindness and extremely grateful for everything done for them. The prayers of pastor and friends in the congregation, for them or for a loved one, were also mentioned frequently as a very important source of support.

The serious illness or death of a loved one was a time of special need for pastoral counseling for many women. It raised questions about the meaning of their own lives and about the nature of God. A pastor able to listen, respond to their needs, and help them deal with issues raised by such traumatic times provided a kind of help that women were not likely to find anywhere else.

Problems with relationships in the family and concern about children's problems also were shared frequently with church members and pastor. However, throughout the churches we visited no consistent pattern as to how much help was received from the church emerged. Some women received strong support while others felt none at all.

Issues regarding their own sexual problems or sexual behavior of children, though often troubling to women, were infrequently dealt with by groups in the congregation and seldom brought to the pastor. In some churches there was recognition of the need for discussing issues of sexuality, but it represented for most people a taboo area. The single, divorced, and widowed women especially felt that their problems in the area of sexuality were not the concern of the church, even though they were searching in their faith for answers to some of these questions.

The other area that was generally felt to be quite separate and distinct from the church was a woman's work. The meaning and responsibilities of being a wife and mother were concerns that might enter the sphere of the church. A woman could expect to find affirmation of the importance of these roles from congregation and pastor, though probably not recognition of some of the feelings of being isolated and undervalued, or other strains of this role.

For employed women, the meaning of a career, the family stress associated with her working, or problems experienced on the job were not usually issues with which she felt the church was concerned. This is not surprising, since many women also shared their feelings of guilt over not doing more work for the church because they had full-time jobs, or their feelings of being isolated from the church after changing from volunteer work to paid work.

Conclusions

Death and illness have always been a part of life's natural transitions. These are familiar, and familiar patterns of dealing with them are in the church. The concerns that are more directly connected with recent changes in society, such as women working outside the home, separation and divorce, and an openness and questioning about norms of sexual behavior are all areas with which the church seems least likely to deal.

New questions are being asked. Searching for the answers is an uncomfortable and sometimes painful process. Women want help working through these issues, and either because they do not feel the issues are within the sphere of the church or because the church does not seem responsive, many are dealing with them alone or taking them elsewhere.

We cannot make the assumption that all of life's concerns should be dealt with in the context of congregational life. It is not necessarily desirable that the spheres of personal concerns and church totally overlap. However, our findings do raise this question, Since a basic faith in God undergirds and informs the way we live and the decisions we make as Christians, how can the church better nurture faith development and assist its members in applying their faith to the everyday issues in their lives?

CHAPTER 5

Implications for the Church

It has been said that the great human drama of the decade of the seventies was women. The story of their lives became the dominant saga of work, life, and marriage. Our interviews in The United Methodist Church continued the vivid themes that the media, film, and literature have placed before us.

We found church leaders surprised by the high degree of energy and excitement that emerged around the discussion of women's lives and issues. We heard time and again personal private stories of the transitions women had experienced. Most participants were actively engaged in church life. Yet, even here at the very core of church activity the interviews uncovered story after story of private, complex, stressful, exciting, and far-reaching changes in the patterns and styles of women's lives. For those who still believe that the "changing role of women" is an artificial media event or that such changes are of little import to the typical woman, our story provides small comfort.

The issues are omnipresent and the church has begun to explore the implications. Women are more involved in positions of leadership and influence, as shown by our study and studies done by other denominations, for example, 1978 Survey, Women's Representation in the Presbyterian Church, U.S. and 1976 Survey, Participation of Women in the American Lutheran Church. The desire is present on the part of church leaders to examine, question, and adjust to this emergent assertive role of women in the church and in society. We found a genuine eagerness to learn and to be responsive. Those who are so searching should direct attention, thoughtful examination, and discussion to some critically important aspects of church life.

Pattern of Pastoral Care and Ministry

The local congregation is expected to be a place of support and help in times of personal crisis. Sanctuary and solace are widely cherished ingredients of congregational life, for both giver and receiver.

One sees a consistent image of love, warmth, and personal care as valued goals and expressions of congregational life. The death of a loved one or severe personal illness quickly kindles their values into a tangible outpouring of warm support. Thus, even for many of the women whose struggles remain private and unnoticed, the sense of support and care still persists. Perhaps analogous to the distant friend or relative whose care and love seem important to us even though the particular personal crisis of the moment remains unknown or unnoticed by them, so the abiding sense of the church as a caring institution seems important to the majority of these women.

The clergy person's style of pastoral ministry and the way it is perceived emerge as crucial and distinctive in shaping the climate of ministry in the congregation. Some women had received specific help from their pastor. Others felt disappointed or rejected by the pastoral response to their needs. Still other women simply felt that the minister was not someone they could turn to for help. What the women have in common is the emphasis placed on the pastor's role and authority in shaping this healing climate. Seemingly this foreground presence of the pastor holds true whatever his or her intent or style of ministry.

Against this backdrop of generalized concern and consolation it is important to review a more unsettling pattern of issues:

—Large, important areas of women's lives remain their private province. Beyond the ministry to the sick, dying, and bereaved there is a surprising lack of intentional pastoral care. The church seldom encounters issues such as sexuality, career change, and sex-role life-style.

—Pastoral counseling, from whatever source, is infrequently utilized as a source of guidance.

—The presence of a female pastor seems to encourage women to seek help more readily and for a wider range of issues.

—Informal groups and relationships are often the source of pastoral help—providing a setting in which to discuss, explore, and seek guidance.

—Many women witness to the strength they have drawn from their personal prayer and devotional life in coping with the stress and strain of personal crises or change.

In addition to the individual questions raised by these tentative findings, their overall pattern suggests some further implications.

Awareness of a Larger Range of Pastoral Issues. The church has centuries of tradition and development behind its pastoral ministry to the ill, to the dying, and to the bereaved. The more hidden crises of life have not received this same attention and hence are not often perceived as crises by the helper or the one receiving help. Despite the new, emergent focus upon life stages, transitions, and the management of stress, our normal assumptions remain largely unchanged. Many difficult and painful issues profoundly affecting women's lives are not shared with the congregation or with clergy because women do not feel they are important enough and because they do not want to bother others unless the issue is critical. This includes concerns as central as changes in their lives that challenge traditional role values, or the confrontation of their children's changing values and life-styles, or the woman's own sexual expression and behavior.

We suggest that it is time to write a new chapter in the history of pastoral care. It is time for ministrations of congregational life to bring into full view all the seasons of life and their expected crises. In the journey from birth to death, whether by accidental life events or from the almost predictable crises that accompany the transition and passage from one life stage to another, the occasions for pastoral care are manifold and profound. Nevertheless, the pastoral care of the church has yet to be shaped to help all of us, male or female, remain aware of and responsive to our own needs, as well as to those of others, in these transitions and crises.

Alternative Models of Care. Our study indicates that the formal and informal groups and relationships so characteristic of congregational life possess a pastoral power of high potential. To listen to the stories these women tell is to realize that much of the help women receive comes from their "network of support"—from the web of friends and colleagues to whom they turn in order to cope with the strain of personal crises.

For the Christian community the intentional development of support systems seems both possible and natural. This peer support is more suited in almost every way to the patterns of parish life than the counseling and therapy model now so widely practiced. Such a pastoral theology and practice of support systems tailored to congregational life and focused on some of the more predictable passages of adult life is an already overdue priority.

A Washington, D.C.-based ecumenical clergy training program for pastors who have made a recent job change helps clergy to:

1. Understand the stress associated with the change of a pastorate
2. Understand their need for support systems
3. Analyze their present means of coping
4. Become productive in the forming of needed support systems

This program has discovered the same pattern of

quiet, often desperate coping, in these ordained men and women that was seen in the lay women of this study. The course has helped them to recognize the crises associated with their move and to mobilize their resources to receive help. Such programs of pastoral care need to be developed for the local congregation.

Our interviews also exposed a second problem inherent in too heavy a reliance on the psychotherapy model of pastoral care. Many women gave eloquent witness to their firm belief that God is active in their lives and a sustaining presence in troubled times. This faith is often coupled with an active devotional life and a strong reliance on personal prayer.

Personal faith is certainly the most basic source of strength and support for a majority of the church women we interviewed. Yet many of them did not directly relate it to their experience or activities in the church. The impression sometimes conveyed was that their faith would exist without their involvement and sometimes almost in spite of their involvement in the church. Spiritual formation and the life of prayer are often seemingly isolated and esoteric aspects of congregational life. Our study indicates that such matters are far more present in the actual life-style of female members than would be indicated by any parish program listings. Again, we believe that a more complete model of Christian pastoral ministry would include both serious attention to intentionality in the development of spiritual and devotional practice and an emphasis on the recognition of personal crises so the individual can mobilize resources for support and help.

The Need to Reexamine Our Present Culture of Theology and Values

Penelope Washbourn has written a book which explores the theological ramifications of feminine life stages. We wish to quote at length from the introduction to her book *Becoming Woman: The Quest for Wholeness in Female Experience* (New York: Harper & Row, 1977) because the point where she begins her book is the focus of our closing summary finding. Dr. Washbourn, a professor of religion at the University of Manitoba, states:

> My conviction is that religious questions and reflections about the meaning of what is holy or ultimate arise at times of crisis in the life of the individual and of the community. These crises may be historical or personal events, but because of them we are forced to respond to a new situation. The question of the meaning of our identity and our attitude toward life is challenged. A crisis is a time of change, anxiety, and possibility. Something new happens, and we summon resources from the past, as well as discover new strengths, to deal with the implications of our changed situation.

Penelope Washbourn could have written this paragraph after hearing the stories of the United Methodist church women in this study. Their transitions and crises are clearly teachable moments for these women. The dilemmas of their lives are certainly periods that give opportunity for reexamining old patterns of values, behaviors, and life-style directions. It must be remembered also that these personal changes are taking place at a moment when American culture is also in transition with regard to many of the issues these women are facing.

The massive dislocation in our cultural norms regarding marriage, divorce, premarital sex, the roles of working women, and the definition of valued feminine attributes can be clearly heard in the stories of the women and in the statements of church leaders. While individual women in one-to-one conversation may paint a fairly consistent picture of quiet coping, the groups with whom we talked could be characterized as quizzical, questioning, searching, and curious about those changing issues and their possible resolution. While some women in the study described themselves as "closet feminists," it is certainly fair to say that the overall mood toward women's issues was of searching indecision.

In light of this search for meaning, what became notable was the lack of opportunity for much dialogue. The women were lonely questioners in their need to find resolution of the issues. The church's ministry of preaching, teaching, and inquiry was seldom mentioned as a source for informing their daily lives. Even around the questions of divorce and remarriage the church emerged as an uncertain mentor, preferring the issue to stay hidden or go away rather than having to assume a position or become involved.

Despite the low visibility of the church's formal teaching ministry, it became apparent that the normal everyday processes and programs of congregational life did convey a message. For instance, the expectation that women will continue to spend the same amounts of time in service to the church as they have in the past is not realistic and is frustrating and guilt-producing for those who are employed and no longer have the time to give. Where there is a single-minded focus on the needs of the institution in terms of finding people to fill jobs, to serve on committees, and to get the work done, it conveys the message that the women are valued to the extent they can fit into a slot, while possibly ignoring their own special interests, experience, and abilities. On the other hand, the presence of a female pastor seems to convey the message that the personal issues of women are important and worthy of consideration, and this helps women share a broader range of concerns.

In a similar fashion, there is an implied message in the lack of talk about the problems of single and divorced women. Though accepting attitudes were expressed toward single and divorced women, there is apt to be a feeling of separation and isolation on their part when most concerns expressed in congregational life are family-oriented and social activities are geared to families. While we found little outright rejection of divorced women, the discomfort of members in recognizing and accepting divorced persons, combined with the woman's own possible sense of failure, lead to a frequent inhibition in her participation in congregational life.

One place where the sharing of important personal concerns did happen was in certain small groups in the church such as prayer groups or other informal groups that met regularly and did not have a closely structured agenda. If a woman's involvement in church activities is limited to attending services, working on committees or structured projects, there is not likely to be an opportunity for either sharing personal needs or discussing issues that relate to dilemmas in her life outside the church.

Along with structuring ways for more sharing, the church can recognize changing needs and realities for women by encouraging them to take the initiative in developing educational programs that speak to current issues in their lives. The church can provide resources to help women mobilize to meet their needs. If groups meet at times inconvenient for older women or employed women, changes in scheduling meetings can be made. The failure to do so is an affirmation that institutional priorities have precedence.

There are many women who will continue to choose the more traditional women's work, will do it well, and will find satisfaction in it. But knowing that they have a real choice and are welcome and accepted in a variety of roles can be very affirming and can convey the message that the individual is important and her needs and wishes are important.

The painful questions raised by the changing lives and roles of women represent an important set of opportunities for the church to engage women in a renewed and deepened awareness of the gospel. We found a readiness for that exploration, which must not be missed.

CHAPTER 6

A Guide for Reflection

The issues we have surfaced in listening to women's stories are but a part of a much broader picture of change and its implications for the church's ministry. Because of the times and the focus on women's lives, the spotlight on women has become an avenue for expressing concerns about how the church is fulfilling its role. However, the basic questions raised in this study are relevant to men, to teen-agers, to children, to pastors, to lay leaders, and to everyone.

As a guide to exploring these issues further, we offer some questions for reflection and discussion in these areas: role of the church, theology and daily life, shared ministry, and church activities.

Role of the Church

Some commonly held concepts are:

- The church is a place of sanctuary and solace.
- It is a community that helps one deal with the more obvious life events, such as illness and death.
- It offers a place and structure for Christians to gather together as a family and to worship God together.
- Belonging to a church makes a statement to the world that one believes in God.

In reality these concepts about the church proved to be limited in meeting the needs of women. Questions related to expanding the understanding of the role are:

1. Does the church's role include dealing with contemporary issues of sexuality, divorce, abortion, equal rights?
2. In what way is the role of the church explored with the congregation?
3. Are church activities examined in the light of what the congregation sees its needs to be?
4. What is the climate and style of pastoral care in the congregation? Is it meeting the needs and expectations of the people it serves?
5. How is the role of the church communicated to the larger community?

Theology and Daily Life

The word "theology," which means "thinking about God," implies for many an intellectual understanding of God, which theologians and clergy interpret *for* laypeople. In looking at the role of the church in women's lives, we see a gap between the "theology of the church" and the personal "knowing God" experienced both in the daily routine of life and in moments of deep need. We see a hungering to relate the message of the gospel to all these needs.

1. What are some ways of linking the promises and demands of the gospel, as revealed in Scripture and the teachings of the church, with the everyday realities of people's lives?

2. How can reflection on the life experiences of people help us better understand God's Word?
3. If times of change and crises present special "teachable moments," how do we know what and when the "teachable moments" are in people's lives? Are we listening to one another?
4. How can the church utilize the opportunity presented in "teachable moments"?
5. What programs, small groups, and resources are offered in congregations to foster spiritual growth?

Shared Ministry

Though the role of the pastor is readily recognized, not only as a preacher of the Word, leader of the congregation, and administrator, but also as a supporter and resource in times of trouble, the role of men and women in the congregation in terms of ministering to each other is less clearly perceived. The women we talked to shared the importance of being helped by others in time of need, but in describing their own church activities they did not often perceive their involvement with others as ministry.

1. How do laypeople and clergy in congregations see their roles and tasks in relation to each other and to the total ministry of the church?
2. Are the ordained clergy perceived as the "real" ministers?
3. How are individual gifts and talents recognized, and how are people encouraged to use them?
4. In light of the need identified for a broader and

deeper pattern of pastoral care and ministry, and the equal reality of overburdened clergy, how can laypeople share more fully in this role?

5. Does the leadership style of both clergy and laypersons allow issues to emerge and help people develop ways of dealing with them?

6. In the training of clergy in seminaries and in congregations, what understanding is formed about their role and the role of the laity?

Church Activities

The pattern of how a congregation provides ways for people to be involved in the church community includes many levels of activities—housekeeping and caretaking functions in the building, work on committees, teaching, and calling—to name a few.

Some of these relate to maintaining the institution as a building and as an organization; others focus on the needs of individual members; still others direct attention to needs outside the church. A look at how all these activities serve the needs of the institution and/or individuals, prompts these questions:

1. How can housekeeping and other necessary-but-draining jobs be done and activities that nourish and energize people be provided?

2. In recruiting people for jobs and activities in the church, is the focus on fitting them to the job or starting with their talents and interests and looking for a job or creating one that suits them?

3. Does overprogramming of activities keep individual needs from emerging and being met?

4. How are clergy responding to women who curtail activities when they seek employment?
5. How are fellow members (men? women?) responding to these women?
6. Are enough opportunities for small groups made available to fill the need for support and in-depth study or sharing?
7. Are groups and activities planned with the needs of particular people in mind, such as single or divorced women, older women, career women, or women with small children?

This is not an exhaustive list; there are more questions to be asked. Some of our questions may imply an answer or assumptions about the issue. They are intended to be provocative and to stimulate thinking about various aspects of the church's life and task. We cannot give answers but hope these questions will guide reflection on issues that profoundly affect the role of the church in people's lives, and will provoke more questions about how the church carries out its task.

Again, the issues springing from talking with women apply to men as well. The perspectives of men may differ from women, but the impact of change in general and changing roles in particular is present in their lives also. Developing ways for the church to respond with sensitivity and a realistic concern for the effects of change in all our lives will require a continuing commitment to learn more about what that change means for individuals and to shape ministry for all people based on that knowledge.